OUT OF GAS ON
LOVERS LEAP

BY MARK ST. GERMAIN

★

★

DRAMATISTS
PLAY SERVICE
INC.

OUT OF GAS ON LOVERS LEAP
Copyright © 1985, Mark St. Germain

All Rights Reserved

SPECIAL NOTE

Anyone receiving permission to produce OUT OF GAS ON LOVERS LEAP is required to give credit to the Author as sole and exclusive Author of the Play on the title page of all programs distributed in connection with performances of the Play and in all instances in which the title of the Play appears for purposes of advertising, publicizing or otherwise exploiting the Play and/or a production thereof. The name of the Author must appear on a separate line, in which no other name appears, immediately beneath the title and in size of type equal to 50% of the size of the largest, most prominent letter used for the title of the Play. No person, firm or entity may receive credit larger or more prominent than that accorded the Author.

SPECIAL NOTE ON SONGS AND RECORDINGS

For performances of copyrighted songs, arrangements or recordings mentioned in this Play, the permission of the copyright owner(s) must be obtained. Other songs, arrangements or recordings may be substituted provided permission from the copyright owner(s) of such songs, arrangements or recordings is obtained; or songs, arrangements or recordings in the public domain may be substituted.

SPECIAL NOTE

Music for the song "At the End of Every Tunnel" is included at the back of this edition and may be used by groups authorized to present OUT OF GAS ON LOVERS LEAP without payment of an additional fee.

OUT OF GAS ON LOVERS LEAP opened at the WPA Theatre, 138 Fifth Ave., New York, on April 23, 1985.

WPA Artistic Director: Kyle Renick
Managing Director: Wendy Bustard
Literary Manager/Casting Director: Darlene Kaplan

Cast:

MYST .... Melissa Leo
GROUPER .... Fisher Stevens

Director — Elinor Renfield
Setting — Edward T. Gianfrancesco
Lighting — Craig Evans
Costumes — Don Newcomb
Sound — Aural Fixation
Stage Manager — Michael S. Mantel
Technical Director — Norman Frith
Property Mistress — Leah Menken
Box Office Manager — Ann Hargraves

NOTE:

The production was performed without an intermission, though an intermission may be taken following Act One. Running time is approximately forty-five minutes per act.

Cast

"GROUPER" (Chauncey) MORRIS—age 17, son of Senator
    Clifford Morris
"MYST" (Mystery) ANGELEEDS—age 17, daughter of rock
    singer Snow Angeleeds

Time

The present.
Night of commencement for senior class of White Oaks Academy, an exclusive boarding school for students with "behavioral disorders."

Place

Eagle Point, overlooking the New England town of Grosset Bay.

OUT OF GAS
ON LOVERS LEAP

ACT ONE

Before lights dim, we see the promontory of Eagle Point; a tree covered parking/lookout area rising above the town of Grosset Bay. A parking barricade at the cliff's edge prevents cars from driving too close to the edge.

A car may or may not be in place, parked, at this point, but must be there when lights rise.

In darkness, we hear the steady, rising roar of the rock song "Dancing With Myself"* and, if car is not yet in place, the sound of the car coming closer.

Lights up reveal a beat up, ancient convertible, top down; its bright yellow body covered with hundreds of bumper stickers applied like bandaids. Many rock groups are touted, and there is an abundance of Bruce Springsteen stickers along with others such as "Nuke The Whales," "Humpty Dumpty Was Pushed," "I Aim For Small Animals," etc.

A Hula Girl figure is mounted on the car's back seat panel. The car's occupants are driver Grouper Morris and Myst Angeleeds. Myst is a striking looking 17 year old with mid-length, multi-colored streaked hair. Grouper, the same age, has shorter hair and wears an earring from his left ear. Both are wearing graduation gowns, open at the front, and graduation caps.

Myst and Grouper are singing with the song, dancing with the song. Grouper climbs over the windshield to stand on the hood.

GROUPER. (*Howling at the moon above, then shouting.*) HEY MOON! Somebody screwed up—we graduated. (*Turns to Myst.*) Give me your hat, Myst—

MYST. Give me your body, Grouper. (*Grouper grabs the hat,*

---

* See Special Note on copyright page.

5

jumps off car and runs to the parking barricade near the cliff's edge, balancing on it.) Careful, you asshole!

GROUPER. (*Holding both graduation caps and slicing the air with them.*) Lethal weapons—(*He mimes throwing them down off the cliff.*) Racing towards Mountain Road—faster, faster—

MYST. Towards two unsuspecting joggers—

GROUPER. Two joggers sliced into four meaty halves—3, 2, 1—(*Grouper winds up to throw.*)

MYST. Don't!

GROUPER. Why not?

MYST. I want my tassle. (*Grabs hat.*) Mr. Percy was right. Our graduation *could* make a difference to the world.

GROUPER. (*Solemnly; wipes his nose with his hand before extending that hand.*) Graduate—

MYST. (*Does the same.*) Graduate. (*They join hands in exaggerated formality. Music on the radio begins to change, and is replaced with a moaning, sensual song with a slower beat.*) AAGHH! (*Myst dives into the car, shutting off the radio.*)

GROUPER. What was that?

MYST. My mother. (*She takes a joint from the dashboard.*)

GROUPER. How could you tell?

MYST. All of her songs have that "I'm almost coming" beat. I can usually shut her off by the first word. If only it was that easy in real life.

GROUPER. (*Pretended puzzlement.*) Real life? Have you been going somewhere without me?

MYST. Grouper; I want my graduation present. You promised.

GROUPER. (*Indicates her joint.*) Are you going to use that or just wave it around all night? (*Myst puts the joint up her nose.*) Wrong stuff.

MYST. No wonder it's so hard to get high. Finished? (*Holds empty beer bottle in hand.*)

GROUPER. Finished.

MYST. Contact.

GROUPER. Contact. (*Both simultaneously toss beer bottles over their shoulders. There is a crash; they turn to look.*)

MYST. Shit.

GROUPER. We can always drive back on the hubcaps.

MYST. You don't have a spare?

GROUPER. You know I don't! We rolled it down Kruger Hill.

6

MYST. That's right.

GROUPER. Good tire, too. It really took off.

MYST. (*Edging closer to him.*) Now how about my graduation present —

GROUPER. I got the newspaper we sent for from Seaside Heights today —

MYST. Is that why you won't sleep with me, Grouper?

GROUPER. (*Ignoring her.*) There are all kinds of jobs down there for the summer. We could work the Boardwalk, or the rides, and there's a million restaurants —

MYST. You're not holding out for another virgin, are you?

GROUPER. (*Stares at her.*) I *do* want to get laid in this lifetime.

MYST. Goddamn right. Besides, if you do it with somebody as dumb as you are about it, the first time will suck. You'll be trying so hard to look pornographic you won't feel a thing. Believe me.

GROUPER. You're the expert.

MYST. Damn right. And I know you. You'll want somebody who will spend more time talking about it afterwards than doing it.

GROUPER. Bullshit.

MYST. No shit. Do yourself a favor. If you decide on somebody else, call me in to coach. We'll see if she has a sense of humor.

GROUPER. So what about us going to Seaside for the summer?

MYST. (*Shrugs.*) How do I know if we're even sexually compatible?

GROUPER. What will really be great is the shore in the winter time.

MYST. Nobody will be there!

GROUPER. That's right. Empty beaches, empty boardwalks — it's the best.

MYST. A ghost town!

GROUPER. Yeah. Guaranteed to be the most romantic time you've ever had. Trust me.

MYST. I don't think ghosts are romantic.

GROUPER. I do. Just think of it. You and I cruising up to the Stone Pony in Asbury Park after we're out all day ice fishing . . .

MYST. ICE FISHING?

GROUPER. We'll have to eat, right? So we'll be in the Stone

Pony, nobody there, except you, me, the bartender and Bruce Springsteen. And I'll say, "Bruce . . .

MYST. "You know that riff you and Clarence do on 'Born In The U.S.A. . . .'

GROUPER. "'Dancing In The Dark? . . .'

MYST. "I think you could goose it up with a little more brass."

GROUPER. And I'll turn to you and say, "Myst —

MYST. "Did you ever sleep with Bruce Springsteen?" (*They kiss.*)

GROUPER. So what about Seaside? It's seventy three degrees down there, sun expected all weekend and the bluefish are running. (*Myst stares at him.*) I called the coastguard.

MYST. (*Evasive.*) Put the radio on. No, never mind — God knows who they're playing. Grouper, I want to ask you a question. And I want you to be honest.

GROUPER. I'll see what I can do.

MYST. Don't you want to sleep with me?

GROUPER. Of course I do! But I want it to be perfect.

MYST. I will be. I always am.

GROUPER. We can do it on the beach, under the full moon —

MYST. And get sand pounded up my ass? No way. Or else I get the top —

GROUPER. I just want to make sure it's historic, that's all.

MYST. It has to be. Because you're one of a kind, and I'm one of a kind.

GROUPER. That makes two of a kind.

MYST. They could never screw up genes this way again —

GROUPER. I know that.

MYST. Do you? Do you think you could ever find somebody like me again?

GROUPER. Do you think you could find somebody like me?

MYST. That's what I mean — who else would drink milkshakes out of my Addidas —

GROUPER. *After* you ran the mile.

MYST. Exactly.

GROUPER. Who else would wear underwear on her head in Calculus and tell Gronk she had to 'cause she had her period?

MYST. Who else would crash the prom dressed like Bonnie and Clyde and hold up the faculty table?

GROUPER. (*Proud.*) *Your* idea —

MYST. But you found the machine gun that worked.

GROUPER. I guess it's a good thing your mom gives White Oaks a lot of money.

MYST. I'll say.

GROUPER. We studied your mother in class.

MYST. Child Psychology?

GROUPER. American Music. Peskow's course. Prehistoric Pop.

MYST. That's funny; I never knew my Pop.

GROUPER. You *really* don't know who your father is?

MYST. I told you that.

GROUPER. No shit?

MYST. Plenty. But it's the truth, too.

GROUPER. It better be. It's graduation night. You have to be truthful — you're an adult now. (*Both adopt serious expressions.*)

MYST. Mr. Morris-Snow told me my egg was in the blender on the tour of '67; so that means Dad was someone from L.A., Denver, Mexico City, New York, Chicago or Boston.

GROUPER. Wow. I wish I didn't know who my father was.

MYST. What was really impressive was the way my mom was so subtle about it.

GROUPER. Naming you "Mystery"?

MYST. That's nothing. There's no limit to her bad taste. She ran a contest in Rolling Stone, "Find Her Father," and she'd do a benefit concert for your school or something. People were hiring detectives, bringing busloads of guys to her, but she was never sure who it was herself. After awhile, everybody gave up.

GROUPER. Needle in the haystack, huh?

MYST. The Disappearing Dick of Mexico City, I think.

GROUPER. Why Mexico City?

MYST. I get homesick when I eat tacos.

GROUPER. You want to see my graduation present from Capitol Hill? (*Takes out a pen and pencil set from the glove compartment.*)

MYST. Super. Couldn't get much more original than that, could they?

GROUPER. (*Unscrews the top of the pen.*) Look. Better than Cracker Jacks.

9

MYST. (*Looking.*) Your folks sent you coke?

GROUPER. Nah. They sent me the pen set and $500. Want some?

MYST. No thanks. I'm protecting this snoz.

GROUPER. (*Indicates hula girl on back dash.*) There's more joints under her hula skirts.

MYST. No wonder she never stops shaking. Grouper, you are a man after my own heart. (*Takes a joint.*)

GROUPER. (*With previously unseen sincerity.*) I am.

MYST. What?

GROUPER. After your heart.

MYST. (*Pause.*) You got it. (*Climbs on hood of car.*) How high up are we?

GROUPER. Me or you?

MYST. Us.

GROUPER. Very.

MYST. Isn't it dumb how they let cars park so close to the edge? Doesn't anyone ever drive off?

GROUPER. Are you kidding? People have respect for their cars. They park here and jump. You should have been here last Christmas —

MYST. (*Quickly, defensively.*) I couldn't be.

GROUPER. (*Pause.*) I know you couldn't.

MYST. (*Lightly.*) So you can lie as much as you want to.

GROUPER. (*Indicates over cliff.*) Guy in one of the houses down there had a fight with his wife over the Christmas tree, right? She said it didn't have enough tinsel on it or some fucking shit. The guy drags it from his living room, lights, decorations and all, throws it on top of his car and drives up here.

MYST. Want a beer?

GROUPER. Yeah. So the guy winds up to toss the tree over the side — guess he wanted to crash it through his roof — just as he throws it over his leg gets caught in a string of lights.

MYST. (*Delighted, looking over cliff.*) Really?

GROUPER. I swear.

MYST. Right over? (*Grouper makes a diving motion.*) Wow!

GROUPER. It was a big goddamn tree.

MYST. Did he splatter?

GROUPER. Let me put it this way. There was a lot more

hanging from that tree than tinsel.

MYST. (*Sings.*) "Oh Christmas Tree, O CHRISTMAS TREE . . .

BOTH. "HOW LOVELY ARE THY BRANCHES."

GROUPER. So Myst—

MYST. So Group—

GROUPER. What do we do with the rest of our lives?

MYST. Number one, we finish these. (*They click beer bottles.*) My mother almost came tonight.

GROUPER. Jesus.

MYST. Her and Roger.

GROUPER. Captain Weave Job? The Man with the Plasticene Hair?

MYST. The one and only. They wanted to fly in from London; imagine that? Every asshole in the school would be hassling them.

GROUPER. Percy's lips would be in traction with all that ass kissing.

MYST. Damn right.

GROUPER. I used to think your mother was pretty hot when I was a kid.

MYST. So did I, until I grew up and she didn't. Barry Zenakus told me he used to have wet dreams about her. Did you?

GROUPER. Probably. I dreamed about anything female. My bed was a swamp.

MYST. Did you lock yourself in the bathroom with a copy of "Playboy"?

GROUPER. Nah. I'd leave it around the living room, especially if Mom and Dad were having company. They threatened to come up tonight, too.

MYST. My mom still looks good from a distance, but once you get up close, forget it. She's flopping all over the place. That's why she's always wearing leather, you know? Holds in the wobble. Really. She has no waist anymore. They build up her hips like Play Doh. I have a much better body. Wait 'till you see.

GROUPER. How did you talk her into not coming for graduation?

MYST. I didn't. I told her it was next week. She's coming Thursday.

11

GROUPER. I told my dad's secretary that if he or Mom showed up I'd phone in a bomb scare.

MYST. Cops wouldn't care. They probably get a dozen a day from this school. They're just hoping for the real thing. Could you believe how many people were taking pictures tonight?

GROUPER. The old fucks wanted proof that their kids graduated.

MYST. So many flash bulbs. When I walked in I thought we were getting nuked. I thought, "Shit. I knew I wouldn't make it."

GROUPER. My father gets off on flash bulbs. Gives him a rush. I think when he and Mom do it they get the press corps in to shoot away and give him incentive.

MYST. They still do it, you think?

GROUPER. I guess. I'm not saying he takes off his suit, but they probably still do it. Doesn't your mother?

MYST. Oh, sure. But that's almost part of her job, you know?

GROUPER. The only person I wish could have been here is Matthew, but somebody would have had to bring him.

MYST. (*Pause; she changes the subject.*) I think the air is thinner up here, don't you?

GROUPER. How about letting my brother visit us once in awhile?

MYST. Sure. You remember our first date? When you stole the movie projector —

GROUPER. (*Cuts in.*) *Borrowed.* It's not stolen 'till they catch you.

MYST. *Borrowed* the copy of "Wizard of Oz," too, and we went up to the library tower roof and beamed it into the sky, drank a case of Moosehead and threw the empties over the side into the faculty parking lot? That was the most romantic night I ever had.

GROUPER. You know much about retarded kids?

MYST. Besides you?

GROUPER. (*Stiffens.*) I'm talking about my brother.

MYST. Oh.

GROUPER. You're going to like Matthew. A lot. He's always smiling, you know — but it's a real smile. Not a professional smile or a smart ass smile but a smile like he's really happy.

MYST. (*Casually.*) You really like kids, don't you?

GROUPER. (*Surprised.*) I guess. But he's not a kid.

12

MYST. You think we should go to Whorrie Laurie's party tonight?

GROUPER. You want to?

MYST. I don't know. It is our graduation.

GROUPER. That's right. Now we start real life.

MYST. You sound so nasty when you say that.

GROUPER. When do we leave for Seaside?

MYST. We don't necessarily have to go to Seaside just to live by the ocean, you know.

GROUPER. What do you mean?

MYST. I'm sure my mother would give us her house at Malibu —

GROUPER. Bite your tongue!

MYST. Why?

GROUPER. First of all, it's not even the same ocean. The Pacific Ocean's for pussies.

MYST. You're crazy.

GROUPER. It is *far* more mellow than the Atlantic.

MYST. Ocean is ocean.

GROUPER. Can you imagine *rides* on the beach at Malibu? Can you picture roller coasters and whips and haunted houses —

MYST. Whips and haunted houses, maybe —

GROUPER. Does the Polar Bear club come out in sub-zero temperature in bathing suits to swim every New Year's Day at Malibu? Shit, if it ever got really cold out there they'd close the state. How can you even mention Seaside Heights and Malibu in the same breath? Seaside Heights is *real*. It's for real people, regular working people. The only thing you work for in Malibu is a tan —

MYST. (*Cutting him off.*) I was at the Malibu house this Christmas.

GROUPER. (*Stopped.*) So?

MYST. My mom, old Leather Stocking, had a Christmas party and invited everybody from the record company, and got stoned to oblivion because a couple of the biggies didn't show. She's not imaginative enough to think they might have families or people they actually liked who they'd rather see that day. Christ, I felt sorry for anybody who had to spend Christmas with us. She sat around petting my hair whenever I got close enough, saying to all these guys, "This is my little girl, would you believe it? This is Mystery." And meanwhile, these guys are eyeing the both of us trying to decide whose bones to jump —

GROUPER. I know whose I would —

MYST. Then jump.

GROUPER. I will.

MYST. I'm waiting.

GROUPER. Have you ever done it in a ferris wheel? The largest ferris wheel on the east coast, on a pier right in the middle of the ocean? They'd stop the thing and look up and see the seat on the top rocking back and forth. That would be a first, even for you.

MYST. My mom bought me a doll for Christmas. One of these antique dolls that cost half a Porche —

GROUPER. Why do I get the impression I'm talking to myself?

MYST. She watched me unwrap it; she was jumping up and down like she was ten years old and I said, "Snow" — because God knows I can't call the woman "Mother" in front of company, "Snow, I think you need this more than I do."

GROUPER. (*Imitating radio transmission.*) This is Earth calling Angeleeds — Earth calling Angeleeds — come in please —

MYST. Funny —

GROUPER. (*Excited.*) I'm getting contact — a transmission from somewhere past Saturn —

MYST. Grouper!

GROUPER. (*Looking at her.*) Success! You *can* hear, you *can* listen. (*He grabs her.*) Then listen harder. (*Pause.*) I love you. More than I ever loved anybody. More than anybody's ever loved anybody. Because I'm totally sure we can be happy together 'till we both die. (*Pause.*) That's it, then. We live together, get married, or I jump off this cliff tonight. Your choice.

MYST. Don't your parents expect you home for the summer.

GROUPER. Probably. They always expect the worst. So?

MYST. (*Pause.*) My mom was talking about maybe going to France for awhile.

GROUPER. (*Pause.*) France?

MYST. Yeah; you know — the Eiffel Tower and drinking on the street?

GROUPER. She's taking you?

MYST. I didn't say I'd go . . .

GROUPER. You'd rather spend the summer with her.

MYST. Of course not! (*Pause.*) But even you have to admit

14

there's a difference between Paris and Seaside Heights.

GROUPER. (*Ice cold.*) Get in the car.

MYST. Where are wc going?

GROUPER. *We* are going nowhere, that's where we're going.

MYST. Grouper — are you driving over the edge?

GROUPER. You'll wish. I'm dropping you at Whorrie Laurie's party. (*Tries to start car, it won't turn over.*) Maybe you'll get lucky if somebody's looking for seconds.

MYST. Oh come on. Stop. This is our night.

GROUPER. Call your mother. Tell her to fly over early *if* you can reach her.

MYST. Did I say I'd go? I never said that.

GROUPER. You thought about it.

MYST. What if I did? What's wrong with that?

GROUPER. If you don't know there's nothing I can tell you. (*Tries car again; only a click is heard.*) Goddamn it!

MYST. You want me to look under the hood?

GROUPER. Watch it, Myst —

MYST. Watch what?

GROUPER. DON'T START YOUR MECHANICAL SU-PERIORITY SHIT AGAIN!

MYST. Grouper, my mother lived with a race car driver! I had to pick up something.

GROUPER. I bet you did.

MYST. Funny.

GROUPER. Your mom lived with everybody. And if she didn't like 'em enough to live with, she just fucked them.

MYST. Hey — beef up those memoirs, right?

GROUPER. I'm not kidding around, Myst. (*Car is not turning over.*) SHIT!

MYST. *You* always want to hear who her latest is. You *subscribe* to "People" for Godsake. (*Begins to get out of car.*) Let me take a look —

GROUPER. Stay in the car!

MYST. But you don't know anything about motors!

GROUPER. STAY IN THE CAR! (*Gets out, tries to open hood and can't. Myst reaches down in car, releases hood lock. Hood pops open. He looks at her, then away, leaning over the engine.*) Goddamn piece of Italian shit. (*Screams over cliff's edge.*) This is it! I'm going Jap next time!

15

MYST. (*Watches him.*) You want me to try to turn it over? (*He looks at her.*) The motor. You watch down there, I'll crank it up here.

GROUPER. (*Grudging.*) All right. (*Myst tries again. Nothing. Grouper kicks the bumper a few more times, looks back in.*) Try again. (*She does; nothing. Grouper screams into the engine.*) WHAT'S WRONG WITH YOU?

MYST. (*Looking at dashboard.*) Ah, Grouper—

GROUPER. I'm concentrating! (*He hits spark plugs with beer can.*) Why do I bother wasting good money on gas?

MYST. If you took that car your father wanted to give you—

GROUPER. Did I ask your opinion about anything?

MYST. I thought guys were supposed to like cars.

GROUPER. Sexist bullshit. Guys with metal between their ears like cars. I *hate* this car.

MYST. You hate every car.

GROUPER. True. I wish I were born two hundred years ago. I swear. How many times did you read about horses having heart attacks on people.

MYST. (*Looking back at dashboard.*) Grouper—

GROUPER. I'm trying to fix it! Would you turn it goddamn over, please?

MYST. Were any of these indicators broken?

GROUPER. No! Of course not! (*Pause.*) What do you mean, "Indicators"?

MYST. The gauges—the dials on the dashboard.

GROUPER. They work fine. Would you turn the key now—

MYST. Group—

GROUPER. MYST! JUST GIVE THE FUCKER GAS, WILL YOU?

MYST. I can't.

GROUPER. WHY NOT?

MYST. You're out of gas.

GROUPER. Huh?

MYST. THERE'S NO FUCKING GAS!

GROUPER. (*Slams hood, wipes off hands.*) Fixed. (*Gets in car.*) Now what is all this shit about France?

MYST. My mom wants me to go. But I said . . .

GROUPER. (*Cutting in.*) Let's get this straight, Myst. Right now, okay? Real straight. . . .

16

MYST. (*Turns away.*) I'll walk back to town for gas —

GROUPER. Didn't you hear what I said before? What's the matter with you?

MYST. Nothing's the matter with me. Why don't you get real? Have a beer or a joint — get control of yourself.

GROUPER. I just asked you to marry me! That was a proposal!

MYST. I don't want to hear it. So I didn't listen.

GROUPER. I knew it!

MYST. I don't want to deal with it right now, okay? Can't I just enjoy my fucking graduation night?

GROUPER. I'm talking the rest of our lives and you're worried about your fucking graduation night?

MYST. (*Angry.*) Couldn't you have just bought me a corsage or something? You kill me, Grouper.

GROUPER. Don't you love me?

MYST. Grouper; we're young. We are. I mean, how can you want to get so serious when neither of us ever even had a *job* yet?

GROUPER. I love you, Myst. More than anyone in the whole world. More than anyone in the whole school. (*Grouper climbs over windshield to hood.*)

MYST. Grouper — what are you doing?

GROUPER. (*Walks slowly down hood towards guardrail.*) Remember me, okay? (*Turns, bounces on hood as if diving board, readying himself.*)

MYST. (*Terrorized.*) Don't — Grouper — GROUPER! (*Grouper leaps, jumping off sideways so that he lands safely on the ground.*) Grouper — You asshole! How dare you do that to me! You stupid bastard!

GROUPER. I'm sorry, Myst. I'm sorry —

MYST. (*Punches him.*) YOU SON OF A BITCH! YOU SHITTY SON OF A BITCH SCUM!!

GROUPER. (*Holding her arms.*) I know — I know — but how did it feel?

MYST. Let go of me!

GROUPER. How did it feel when you thought I was jumping?

MYST. I was scared! I hated you. I missed you. (*She pulls free.*) This is to get back at me for Christmas, isn't it?

GROUPER. No — not at all —

MYST. Damn right it is. For me going away and leaving you here —

17

GROUPER. That has nothing to do with it —

MYST. (*Getting more and more upset.*) I tried to call! Every day I did! I called your house, and they never told me a thing — I never knew 'till I got back here . . .

GROUPER. I know that.

MYST. Grouper, you cannot do this to me. You can't love me this much! I can't handle it!

GROUPER. I can't help it, Myst. I swear to God.

MYST. Oh Grouper. You don't believe in God. (*Hugs him.*)

GROUPER. That's not my fault.

MYST. You are the worst thing that ever happened to me.

GROUPER. I wish I didn't care about you, Myst. I really do. I wish I could spit in your face and never see you again.

MYST. Get in the car. (*They do, arms around each other.*) Kiss me. (*He does.*)

GROUPER. To me it's all simple. I see my parents and they're fucked up. I see your mother and she's fucked up. Everybody I know who's gone after things like money and magazine covers all get fucked up. You don't *need* that. All I want is one little thing, Myst. I want to be happy.

MYST. That's not a little thing, Grouper.

GROUPER. You know what my father told me six thousand, seven hundred and fifty-two times? The only intelligent thing the guy ever said, so he said it a lot. He'd say, "Chauncey —

MYST. (*Cutting in.*) "Chauncey." Christ!

GROUPER. "There's only one way to get what you want in this world. Go after it with your life. Live for it. Be ready to die for it." And he's right. Even though *he's* so dumb he's wasting *his* life as a third rate handshaker who's not even sneaky enough to make it to Vice-President.

MYST. Grouper, everybody wants to be happy. Everybody tries to be —

GROUPER. But they don't work at it, Myst. They get side-tracked. I'm working on it; I'm planning for it. We work for just enough money to live on, right, and if one of us works in a restaurant we can even cut down on food costs. We'll lay on the beach all summer and relax — no pressures, no problems. We'll take long walks, there's miles of beach, and if we walk south there's a park, Island Beach State Park, and there's a bird sanctuary. We can go there if we feel like getting away — just the two of us.

MYST. And if *we* have any kind of problem, one of the two of us, what then? Go down to the beach and bitch to the birds?

GROUPER. We talk to each other.

MYST. Talk. Just like that, right? Work it out calmly and rationally. Like you did at Christmas —

GROUPER. I thought you didn't love me and nothing was worth it anymore —

MYST. So you'd stick it to me *and* your father, one shot, right?

GROUPER. My father?

MYST. Ripping up your state flag and tying pieces of it together to hang yourself with —

GROUPER. You know I don't wear belts —

MYST. You walked all the way 'cross campus to the gym! You could have borrowed a belt from somebody —

GROUPER. There was nobody on campus! Everybody was on vacation. I had to break into the gym. Let's not start in on it, okay?

MYST. No; it's not okay. I should listen to a guided tour for happiness from a guy who strung himself up from a basketball hoop? Why would you hang yourself from a basketball hoop?

GROUPER. Myst —

MYST. You could have swallowed pills or sat in the car with the motor running —

GROUPER. This is a convertible!

MYST. Then why the gym? Why not your room or a tree or something? Why pick the gym to hang yourself in?

GROUPER. I don't know. (*Pause.*) It seemed kind of . . . athletic.

MYST. Bullshit. Tell me why. If you love me, Grouper, tell me why.

GROUPER. (*Pause.*) I wanted to get the scoreboard lit up, you know how they do it at the games? But I couldn't get the power on. I wanted it to say "Visitors 1, Home Team, Zip."

MYST. (*Laughs; he laughs with her.*) What did your parents say when Percy called them?

GROUPER. They didn't know much at first. Percy called them Christmas Eve. Told my Dad, "Chauncey had a bit of an accident on the basketball court today . . ."

MYST. (*Laughing.*) He said that?

GROUPER. (*Continuing as Percy.*) "I'm afraid the boy missed the basket, Senator. Landed on his head, he did. Is there anyone you could send up to keep an eye on him?"

MYST. Who came?

GROUPER. Nobody. I told them to stay away. And they did.

MYST. It must have been horrible being in the infirmary on Christmas.

GROUPER. Better than being home. Watching Dad dress up like Senator Santa and visit hospitals and stuff. You know, one year I had to go with him and be an elf! He ho-ho-d himself into the psycho ward by mistake. Yelled out this drippy "Merry Christmas" at the top of his lungs. And all through the hall, you heard this big sound coming back like a wave, "Fuck You!" After that, he'd only go onto the floors where the kids weren't big enough to talk. (*Pause.*) We would have had a great Christmas together. This is Currier and Ives country up here. You know, running around shopping . . . (*Poses in typical card-like style, with huge smile.*) or skating (*Does ice skating pond.*) or Christmas Caroling. (*Poses, then still smiling, gives the finger.*) We could have rented a horse and sleigh or dogsled or something. And we will. Next year.

MYST. What if we have kids. (*He looks at her.*) You ever think of that?

GROUPER. We haven't even had sex!

MYST. When we do.

GROUPER. We'll spend so much time with them they'll beg us to leave them alone, and after that we'll start nagging for grandchildren.

MYST. Grouper — is what happened to your brother . . . hereditary?

GROUPER. No. It was just something that . . . happened. Odds. If I believed in God I'd say spite. But since there's no God there's just . . . math.

MYST. It must have really been hard on all of you.

GROUPER. I don't know. I was so little. I mean, he was only two years younger than me, and I was so happy to have somebody to play with. I never knew there was anything wrong. By

20

the time I grew up, they had enough time to realize the kid's campaign potential, you know? Poster boy time.

MYST. What about your mom?

GROUPER. Mom was always away speaking at these handicapped dinners where half of 'em had a hard time hitting the plate with their fork. First she'd take Matthew, but when he got older, old enough to be a pain in the ass and not as "cute" anymore, she'd just take his picture. And the Senator, he had all kinds of portraits made up. Some of them had Matthew in them and some didn't. So I asked him, "Dad, isn't Matthew going to be in all our pictures?" And he said, "Everything depends on the kind of audience you want to reach, son." Like some voters could believe that people could be retarded, and some couldn't. (*Pause.*) We don't have to have kids, if you don't want to. Hell, I haven't planned much about *that* yet.

MYST. (*Uncomfortable.*) You haven't?

GROUPER. Nah. We don't even have to get married; we can live together.

MYST. (*Relaxing again.*) I don't know. Everybody's getting married now. My mom says you have more fun sleeping around if you're married.

GROUPER. I love your hair. (*He pulls her closer.*) I love the inside of your ear; it looks like a shell, all white and slippery. I'd like to slide up and down in there. (*Nuzzles into her ear.*)

MYST. The tongue — watch the tongue — I'll go deaf —

GROUPER. Huh?

MYST. I said . . .

GROUPER. (*Hand to ear.*) Huh?

MYST. (*Laughs.*) Grouper, do we really have to ice fish?

GROUPER. Not if you don't want to.

MYST. I don't.

GROUPER. Then we won't.

MYST. I don't want to be a waitress, either. I don't want to pick up people's plates and find gum underneath. And if somebody stiffed me I'd carry a gun —

GROUPER. We can get any kind of job we want.

MYST. Anything?

GROUPER. Anything.

MYST. (*Pause.*) We can sing.

21

GROUPER. What?

MYST. If we got some kind of act together, the two of us, we could get some bookings with my name and all . . .

GROUPER. You want to be a singer? A rock singer?

MYST. We can make some quick bucks. Take the money and run.

GROUPER. If you like to sing so much how come you never joined Glee Club?

MYST. I'm not going to sing for nothing. My Mom always wanted me to sing with her when I was a little kid, the Judy and Liza bit, but I never would since she wanted me to so much. Once guys started coming on to me she stopped asking. But she still thinks I have a good voice. I can tell by the way she sneaks looks at me when I do sing.

GROUPER. I kind of wanted to work on a bait boat.

MYST. I could go solo. (*Myst has Grouper's attention again.*) But this would be so much easier. We'd both have our days free, sing a couple of hours, drink free and go home and screw. Screw on the beach, maybe.

GROUPER. Yeah?

MYST. It will be fabulous. There's a lot of bars at the Jersey Shore, aren't there? There *must* be.

GROUPER. I don't know. I've never been there.

MYST. Yeah, but you've done more research on that place than you ever did for anything at School. "Shrine of Springsteen." Anyhow, maybe after we play a few bars we can get a gig in Atlantic City—

GROUPER. Atlantic City? Wait a minute, Myst! Next thing you'll have us opening for Barry Manilow!

MYST. Look; I don't want to get a real job! This would be fun!

GROUPER. Forget it—

MYST. I know you play the guitar—

GROUPER. No way.

MYST. You could be just like Bruce.

GROUPER. (*Pause.*) He sings better than I do.

MYST. That's not always a plus. Okay, if you don't want to sing you can just play. Or write songs for us. We can do all original songs.

GROUPER. I don't even read music.

MYST. You don't have to. Do what I do. Sing them into a tape recorder and we'll pick them up from there.

GROUPER. You write songs? You never told me that.

MYST. I'm not saying they're good. But I do. All the time in my head.

GROUPER. How many other things haven't you told me?

MYST. They just come to me, like they come to my mom. It's almost spooky it's so easy for her. You know her song "Pain Patrol"?

GROUPER. Sure.

MYST. She told me the whole thing came to her when she was waiting on the table at her gynecologists. The whole song in one visit. But she lets everybody think it's about the destruction of the sixties.

GROUPER. Wow.

MYST. And that song "Hot And Heavy"—

GROUPER. Yeah.

MYST. Remember that fat drummer that used to tour with her?

GROUPER. Joey B. or something like that?

MYST. (*Nods her head.*) Right. One night the air conditioning at their Holiday Inn broke down . . .

GROUPER. Christ.

MYST. You know what I hate about her? She's always asking my opinion of her boyfriends. I mean, really. I tell her, "Mom, these guys are scum. Try an accountant or something." But she's so dumb. She thinks people have to be weirder than her to be interesting. And no matter who I bring home, she thinks they're great.

GROUPER. Thanks.

MYST. Come on; you know she liked you best of anybody.

GROUPER. She thought I was weird.

MYST. Of course she did! We're in Squirrel Oaks, aren't we? What else would she expect? Grouper, if you want to live in Springsteen land, I want a band.

GROUPER. I don't know, Myst. You don't want to end up like your Mom, do you?

MYST. I never will. I'm smarter than her.

GROUPER. So what? I'm smarter than my father, but I'm not going to run for Mayor of Seaside Heights.

MYST. I wrote a song about you.

GROUPER. You did?

MYST. You want to hear it?

GROUPER. Of course I do.

MYST. You'd better not laugh.

GROUPER. I won't.

MYST. I want you to like it. Tell me you like it even if you don't.

GROUPER. Lie to you? On the first night of our new lives together?

MYST. Then just be non-committal. Say it's really great, but it needs work.

GROUPER. Okay, sing it.

MYST. You're positive you want to hear it—

GROUPER. I'm positive!

MYST. Then we make a deal.

GROUPER. (*Pause.*) What deal?

MYST. You get what you want if I get what I want. (*Edges closer to him.*)

GROUPER. (*Pause.*) Let's hear how much work the song needs.

MYST.* (*Sings.*)
WHEN THE WORLD IS GETTING DARKER
AND MY DAYS SEEM LIKE MY NIGHTS
WHEN I JUST CAN'T TELL THE DIFFERENCE
FROM MY WRONGS OR FROM MY RIGHTS
WHEN I CLOSE MY EYES UP TIGHT
'CAUSE THERE'S JUST NOTHING LEFT TO SEE
THAT'S THE TIME YOU TOOK FOR COMING
YOU TOOK FOR COMING AFTER ME

AT THE END OF EVERY TUNNEL
THERE'S A LIGHT, THERE'S A LIGHT
AT THE END OF EVERY TUNNEL
YOU'RE MY LIGHT

GROUPER. It's a classic. That is the most instant classic I have ever heard in my life.

MYST. Do you like it?

GROUPER. It's better than Van Halen, or Def Leppard—it's the greatest song ever written!

* Music for this song is included at end of playbook.

MYST. With an electric guitar it will sound a lot better —
GROUPER. It's better *now* than Madonna or Mozart or Twisted Sister. It's better than Bruce!
MYST. Really?
GROUPER. I swear. And it was written for me?
MYST. Is it better than my mother?
GROUPER. Oh yeah. (*She kisses him.*) You sound a little like her, though. But better.
MYST. Really?
GROUPER. Lot's better. (*They kiss.*) You're a lot hotter.
MYST. Now I get what I want —
GROUPER. WAIT! (*Pause.*) This is where people fuck up. Doing things before they make a logical decision about what they should be doing.
MYST. Like killing themselves?
GROUPER. Huh?
MYST. Did you do a lot of thinking about killing yourself?
GROUPER. Sure I did.
MYST. Then you knew pieces of an old flag wouldn't hold you up. And you knew the hoop would tear off once you started shaking around on it —
GROUPER. I didn't think *that* much about it.
MYST. Maybe you did. Subconsciously.
GROUPER. No. I don't have a subconscious, that's my problem. I'm all conscious.
MYST. Then why didn't you jump off the cliffs here?
GROUPER. I figured I'd land on somebody's Christmas tree! (*She laughs, he does too, then stops.*) I would though, Myst. Jump. For you.
MYST. (*Pause.*) I'd jump after you.
GROUPER. You would? Really?
MYST. Yeah. I would.
GROUPER. That's a long way down.
MYST. I know it.
GROUPER. You'd get a lot more than a concussion and stitches from here, you know. We're talking . . . splat.
MYST. I know that.
GROUPER. There's nothing better than you and me, Myst. Marry me.
MYST. Kiss me. (*They kiss.*) You have the greatest mouth.

25

GROUPER. We'll work everything out tonight. Our whole lives —
MYST. Everything.
GROUPER. (*Stopping her kiss; almost threatening.*) We'd better. You promised. (*Myst pulls away a bit, looks at him. Grouper kisses her. Myst and Grouper begin to undress each other; slowly sinking more and more into the car's front seat.*) Wait! (*Grouper takes out a cassette tape, puts it into the tape system. Bruce Springsteen's rendition of Tom Waits' "Jersey Girl"* can be heard.*) I love you, Myst.
MYST. I love you, Grouper.
GROUPER. (*Sinking out of sight.*) We're not going to fuck it up, are we?
MYST. We're going to be great. We're going to be the best. (*They sink out of sight in the front seat. Only their words can be heard as light fades.*)
GROUPER. You're beautiful . . .
MYST. So are you —
GROUPER. Myst —
MYST. Yeah?
GROUPER. Remember what you said about your song — before you sang it?
MYST. What?
GROUPER. You can lie to me.
MYST. I won't have to.
GROUPER. Wow. (*Pause.*) Happy graduation.
MYST. Happy graduation. (*Long pause.*) Grouper . . . you have such a mouth . . . (*One arm can be seen coming up from the front seat; one brightly colored pair of underpants is hung from the rearview mirror. There is a pause. A second pair, even more brightly colored, is hung from the rearview mirror. Volume of song on the tapedeck rises. Blackout. Possible intermission.*)

*See Special Note on copyright page.

ACT TWO

Lights up reveal Myst and Grouper stretched out on the convertible's hood, passing a joint back and forth. They are wearing only their underwear and their graduation gowns, half buttoned, worn like bathrobes.

MYST. (*Long pause.*) I can't believe you lasted that whole tape.
GROUPER. (*Pleased, but surprised himself.*) Yeah. And Percy's always telling me I have no self control.
MYST. Score one for the Home Team.
GROUPER. I'm the Visitors.
MYST. That's right. (*Grouper slides over closer, putting a leg over hers.*) Grouper, give it a rest, will you? Here — (*Hands him the joint.*)
GROUPER. You know something? It *was* historic.
MYST. I'll say.
GROUPER. The only problem is that there can't be a first time again.
MYST. You'll get over it.
GROUPER. I'm running out of firsts.
MYST. It gets even better.
GROUPER. Impossible.
MYST. You'll see.
GROUPER. It's better than drugs.
MYST. That's why you do so much and I don't.
GROUPER. So when do we leave?
MYST. We have to get gas.
GROUPER. We can walk down to Sadowski's *Shell*. It's open all night. (*Gets on his side.*) What do you say we leave tonight? Get on the turnpike and we can watch the sun come up on the beach. It's beautiful.
MYST. It's early.
GROUPER. We won't go to sleep; you won't have to get up. Shit, I don't think I'm going to sleep for days.
MYST. You don't want to go to Laurie's party, then?
GROUPER. I never wanted to. Why should we?
MYST. Isn't there anybody you want to say goodbye to?
GROUPER. I said goodbye to most of those assholes when I

27

said hello. I don't want to see them anymore. This is a new start —

MYST. Start out with a bang, right?

GROUPER. You know something, Myst? I feel really good. The minute Percy handed me that diploma —

MYST. You shouldn't have kissed him.

GROUPER. He had such a "I'm so glad to get rid of this one" look on his face I had to do something. I don't think he ever forgot that machine gun.

MYST. Well, I'd say your kissing him on the feet tonight pissed him off even more.

GROUPER. You laughed, didn't you? (*Looks at her.*) Are you feeling okay?

MYST. Yeah. I'm a little tired. (*Pause.*) And my stomach's been kinda funny lately.

GROUPER. This is the start of life number two: Grouper Morris, Adult. Grouper Morris, Republican.

MYST. Grouper, you're doing it again.

GROUPER. What?

MYST. Setting yourself up to get kicked in the balls. You do it all the time. You get so worked up wanting something to be perfect that when it isn't you get all pissed off and break things and get everybody hating you. You *know* you're going to make mistakes. You're not even 18 yet. You have at least fifty years of mistakes to make, and you're going to make at least one a year.

GROUPER. That's what you think, huh?

MYST. That's the way it always is with you. Isn't that why you're in Squirrel Oaks to begin with?

GROUPER. (*Stares at her.*) Why have I been wasting Dad's money on a psychiatrist all these years? I think you've cleared up my whole life! If only I had met you before I cherry bombed my first Mister Softee truck . . .

MYST. Fuck you.

GROUPER. You're missing the whole point, Myst. That's the way I was before, when I wasn't happy about anything. This is a whole new shot.

MYST. I just don't like you getting so hurt when things don't work out. That's all.

GROUPER. What won't work out? Tell me, Doctor. Better

28

yet, tell me why they put you in the zoo for rich preppies to begin with.

MYST. (*Shrugs.*) I gave too many people shit who weren't paid enough to take it. My mom probably figured putting me here was cheaper. (*She stretches.*)

GROUPER. You have the greatest midriff I have ever seen. Do that again.

MYST. Isn't it getting cold up here? Maybe we should put some clothes on. (*They begin to dress.*)

GROUPER. When you wore those tube tops to class I would get so excited that my desk would rise up twelve inches off the ground—

MYST. Try a six inch hop.

GROUPER. You try it.

MYST. I did. (*Grins.*) I know the difference.

GROUPER. (*Colder.*) That's right. I forgot. You've tried it all, haven't you? All shapes, sizes, colors and flavors, right?

MYST. See that! There you go.

GROUPER. What?

MYST. Your whole new adult life. Starting fresh, starting happy. You're already screwing it up by getting jealous again. I can't stand that.

GROUPER. You're right. It's stupid. No more negative emotions. All gone.

MYST. Oh really?

GROUPER. That's right.

MYST. Never again?

GROUPER. Never.

MYST. (*Pause.*) What if we're on the beach at Seaside and some guy's giving me the eye?

GROUPER. I'll be doing the same thing; I won't see him.

MYST. What happens if we're singing at some bar, and we get a break and they turn on the jukebox and some guy asks me to dance?

GROUPER. You'll dance with him. If you want to.

MYST. Say I want to.

GROUPER. Then you do.

MYST. For more than one dance.

GROUPER. Hey; I'm not going to be possessive like that.

MYST. Good. What if I want to sleep with him.

GROUPER. (*Pause.*) Are we married or what?

MYST. Would it make any difference if we were married?

GROUPER. Wouldn't it to you?

MYST. I asked you first.

GROUPER. (*Lightly.*) If we were the most important people in the world to each other . . .

MYST. (*Cuts in.*) We'd let the other person have the freedom to do what they wanted.

GROUPER. Maybe they wouldn't want to . . .

MYST. Okay. Imagine we're married. Big wedding on the Queen Elizabeth. Honeymoon in Aruba. Or Niagra Falls. That would be really beat.

GROUPER. How about Alaska? I always wanted to see Alaska.

MYST. Fine. So we have a hell of a time watching glaciers and Kodak Bears—

GROUPER. Kodiak.

MYST. We come back to Seaside Heights. First weekend we're here, Nastasia Kinski comes to visit—

GROUPER. You know Nastasia Kinski?

MYST. No, but you wish I did.

GROUPER. Oh yeah?

MYST. How many times did we see "Cat People"?

GROUPER. Go on.

MYST. Nastasia's dropped in—

GROUPER. Right.

MYST. You guys are out in the ocean, swimming around—

GROUPER. I can't swim.

MYST. You want to ice fish and you can't swim?

GROUPER. Why bother? You fall in and you freeze to death whether you swim or not.

MYST. Nastasia wants to swim. You learn in two and a half minutes. You and she are paddling around, splashing each other, playing submarine, and I'm on the beach, getting burned to a blister. Nastasia swims up to you, puts her arms around you, looks right in your face with those big thyroid eyes of hers and says, (*Imitating accent.*) "Grouper, let's do it."

GROUPER. In the water?

MYST. She pushes her smooth, wet body up against yours and opens her big, wide mouth—

GROUPER. I wouldn't do it.

MYST. Why not?

GROUPER. It wouldn't be fair to you.

MYST. I don't want her. Are you trying to tell me you don't?

GROUPER. Sure, but . . .

MYST. Then I give you permission. Anytime, with anyone. That, Grouper, is love.

GROUPER. I'd feel guilty.

MYST. That's another thing you have to get over. Guilt. It's Middle Ages. It's wasted emotion. Don't ever feel guilty. Because I won't. (*Pause.*) Are you O.K.?

GROUPER. Sure.

MYST. You don't seem it.

GROUPER. I'm handling it, aren't I?

MYST. Still want to get married?

GROUPER. Of course I do. (*Pause.*) Let's go get gas; then we can take off.

MYST. (*Uncomfortable.*) Go down the shore?

GROUPER. Yeah. (*Pause.*) Myst; what are you afraid of?

MYST. Let's face it, Grouper. You and I aren't the most normal, easygoing people in the world, you know—

GROUPER. We love each other, don't we? We can make everything work out. Didn't I just let you sleep with some fucking bonehead you haven't even met?

MYST. You got Nastasia Kinski—

GROUPER. (*Holding her.*) Why don't we try the back seat this time? We can get real acrobatic.

MYST. Grouper, I'm not going to promise you my whole life if you don't promise me something, too.

GROUPER. Anything. What?

MYST. You won't try to kill yourself again.

GROUPER. I swear to God!

MYST. You don't believe in God.

GROUPER. Who do you want me to swear to?

MYST. Swear to your brother Matthew. Swear to him . . . and don't hope to die.

GROUPER. I swear to Matthew I'll never try to kill myself again.

MYST. No matter what happens to us.

GROUPER. No matter what.

MYST. No matter what kind of shit I give you.

GROUPER. I'll deal with it. No sweat. I promise.

MYST. What about my mother coming to visit?

GROUPER. (*Pause.*) Your mother?

MYST. (*Defensively.*) If we're moving down the shore and she flies in next week I'll have to at least invite her to visit. Are you going to be able to handle it?

GROUPER. Hell yeah.

MYST. You're sure?

GROUPER. (*Looks in other direction, as if catching something out of the corner of his eye.*) Look — isn't that a Pink Rolls? With hubcaps in the shape of records? That's the first I've seen in Seaside all day . . .

MYST. (*Not anxious to play.*) She'd fly in, Grouper. She wouldn't drive from England.

GROUPER. She must have rented it from Avis, then. It is her! Hello, Myst's mother. I'm sorry. Miss Angeleeds. How nice to see you. You look great — what kind of leather *is* that jumpsuit? Rattle Snake? Terrific; you can get rid of your drummer! (*To Myst.*) Say hello to your mother, Mystery. Don't be rude — you're a Squirrel Oaks Graduate.

MYST. (*Begins to play along, though not enthusiastic.*) Hi, Snow.

GROUPER. (*Imitating Snow. We have the impression that they have played this game many times before.*) Missy! How you doing and who you screwing? Give me a wet one. (*Grouper leans down to kiss her from his standing position on the front seat.*)

MYST. Mother! Don't french!

GROUPER. (*Pulls free; hyperkinetic.*) So much shit coming down, Missy.

MYST. It's MYST, Snow. Missy sounds like "Little Women."

GROUPER. The Captain wants me to sing with him on his new album. I told him, "Honey, it just doesn't feel right to me. I can make this throat sing but not the rest of me, you know?"

MYST. Cut the shit, Snow. Why won't you do it?

GROUPER. Well, he did his last album with Linda and before that with Bette and I just don't want to be another pretty pair of tits to sell an album cover, you see what I'm saying?

MYST. Sure, Snow. I see.

GROUPER. Do you like the Captain, Missy? Tell the truth, really now. What kind of vibes do you get from him.

MYST. No vibes, Snow. I think the Captain is vibe-less. Sometimes, though, I get strange reflections when the light hits his hair. Mom—

GROUPER. MOM! (*Looks around as if embarrassed.*) You don't have to call me *that*, we have a better relationship than *that*, don't we?

MYST. Sure, Snow. (*Looks away; puts her finger down her throat.*)

GROUPER. So tell me, Missy. Are you and this (*Distastefully.*) politician's boy living together? Tell me everything, now. I don't want to read about it first in some supermarket line.

MYST. We are planning to cohabitate, Snow. We're just taking it day by day.

GROUPER. (*Leans into her.*) Is he good? I mean is he . . . (*Mimes gigantic penis size.*)

MYST. *Before* he gets excited.

GROUPER. You lucky girl.

MYST. That's nothing. I've seen some things behind zippers that should be behind bars.

GROUPER. My manager got a call from an old friend at the Chatterbox bar on your boardwalk here. He said you were going to be singing there! I said, "I don't know *what* this man is on, but my little girl doesn't sing . . ."

MYST. It's true, Mother.

GROUPER. Isn't that a scream. (*Pause.*) What name are you using?

MYST. The one you gave me. It's great because it's really memorable.

GROUPER. So. You're following in your (*Pause.*) idol's footsteps.

MYST. No I'm not—

GROUPER. Don't tell the one who gave you the feet they're not my footsteps. Give me a backrub, Missy. Come on, do it now, I'm knotting.

MYST. Snow—

GROUPER. Rub! (*Myst reluctantly massages Grouper's neck.*)

MYST. I'm going to sing my own songs.

GROUPER. I'm *sure* that's why people would come.

MYST. I'm good. I am. You wait and see.

GROUPER. My name, MY act? Honey, I don't see anything but me. (*Myst takes her hands away.*) DON'T STOP! (*Pause.*) I

33

need you. (*Myst rubs again.*) Fabulous, wonderful, keep it up.

MYST. Mom—

GROUPER. SHH! Talk with your fingers. Make yourself good for something.

MYST. You should come and see me—

GROUPER. I'll be out of town.

MYST. But I didn't even tell you when!

GROUPER. (*Turns on her.*) STOP YOUR WHINING! (*Slowly.*) I won't be there. You're a mirror, honey, a fucking mirror. And you know what they'll see when I'm *not* there? (*Pause.*) Nothing.

MYST. (*Pulling away; standing up and looking in the distance.*) Look at that!

GROUPER. What?

MYST. A black Lincoln with an American flag flying from the radio antennae and a license plate that says . . . M . . . O . . . R . . . Morris!

GROUPER. (*As Snow.*) I don't see it; do you see it, Grouper?

MYST. Definitely.

GROUPER. (*As himself.*) I don't see it.

MYST. Listen to the horn.

GROUPER. (*Anticipating.*) Oh God—

MYST. (*Imitates horn beeping "Hail To The Chief."*) Don't you think you'd better be going now, Mom? You've been here five whole minutes—

GROUPER. (*As Snow.*) I want to stay—

MYST. You never want to stay—

GROUPER. (*As himself.*) Let her stay!

MYST. (*Imitating Senator Morris.*) SON!

GROUPER. (*As himself.*) Shit.

MYST. (*As herself.*) Bye, Snow—

GROUPER. (*As Snow, to Senator.*) Hi—I'm Snow Angeleeds—

MYST. (*As Senator.*) So what? (*As herself.*) She's going.

GROUPER. (*Petulantly, as Snow.*) I'm going—

MYST. (*As herself.*) She's gone. (*As Senator.*) CHAUNCEY!

GROUPER. Hi.

MYST. How in hell are you?

GROUPER. Haven't been playing basketball, if that's what you mean.

MYST. (*Laughs heartily.*) Always pulling my leg! How was graduation?

GROUPER. Successful for them. They got rid of me.

MYST. You liked the pen set? Those are Presidential Commemorative Pens, son. Those are the pens the President used when he got Michael Jackson's autograph. You like his music, son? I love it. (*Sings; moving stiffly.*) "Beat It . . ."

GROUPER. The pen set came in real handy.

MYST. Will be of real use to you in a real school. You thought more about college?

GROUPER. (*To Myst.*) That's tape twenty seven. Fast forward. (*Myst imitates a tape going at a fast speed, garbled, then stops suddenly.*)

MYST. . . . responsibility. Son, we should have a little man-to-man before your mother and brother come up.

GROUPER. They're here? You brought the trailer?

MYST. Mother's in the car listening to Doctor Ruth on the radio. They're talking about social diseases, and you know how socially conscious your mother is.

GROUPER. I want you to meet somebody, Dad—

MYST. (*Checks watch.*) I can work it in in five minutes. Now let's not beat around the bush, son. I want to know who's on first and where second is. So far, you've been screwing up your life and doing a good job of it. Between the drugs and getting arrested and thrown from one school to another, you're a class A-1 Juvenile Delinquent. Now what's this I hear about a rumor you've grown up?

GROUPER. No comment. I have no confirmation at this time. (*Trying to interrupt the game.*) Dad, this is Myst Angeleeds—

MYST. (*Pretends to meet her.*) Great Bod. Hell of a lot better looking than her mom. Now, Chauncey, what I want you to do is come down and work for me in Washington this summer as a page—

GROUPER. You're not even in session!

MYST. Then it will be a short page! (*Laughs uproariously at himself.*) Meanwhile, we can talk to some people about getting you into a college even if it isn't first rate.

GROUPER. Hey, neither am I, right, Dad? Fuck you.

MYST. (*Laughs, shakes head.*) You've grown up all right, Chauncey. Are you still pissed at your old man for not allowing you to go to that druggy dry out house? Let them use you as their mascot to get federal funding?

GROUPER. (*Big, unconvincing.*) NOOOOO!

35

MYST. You didn't need it, Chauncey. Look how well you did at White Oaks here. A new school was all you needed—

GROUPER. A new school and a bigger allowance. Why don't you send Matthew up and you guys wait in the car.

MYST. This isn't a very adult way to handle things, is it, Chauncey? Can't you talk it over, man to man?

GROUPER. I don't think you're up for it, Dad. Man to man or person to person. Maybe person to wall.

MYST. (*Hearty laugh.*) You know, son. You never let up. You have a real talent there; you're a wonderful hater. You really are. Except one of these days you're going to run out of people to hate and you'll shrivel up like a used rubber.

GROUPER. I don't have to worry as long as you're around, Dad.

MYST. No, Chauncey. Lucky for you. That way you don't have to look at yourself.

GROUPER. (*Stops playing.*) What do you mean by that, Myst?

MYST. Why don't I get the wife and the poster boy—

GROUPER. I'M SERIOUS, MYST. What did you mean by that?

MYST. Chauncey—

GROUPER. I'M TALKING TO *YOU*. WHAT DID YOU MEAN?

MYST. (*Stops.*) Grouper; we're only playing.

GROUPER. You meant that.

MYST. You started the whole thing.

GROUPER. You think I hate *everybody*?

MYST. Group, you do!

GROUPER. Not you!

MYST. But what happens when we get to the point you do?

GROUPER. That could never happen. Never.

MYST. Why not?

GROUPER. Because I . . . (*About to say "Love You."*)

MYST. DON'T SAY THAT AGAIN! Tell me why.

GROUPER. Because . . . you're the only friend I have.

MYST. (*Pause.*) If I told you I was going to France this summer with my mother, you'd hate me then.

GROUPER. (*Pause.*) You told her you'd go, didn't you.

MYST. Pretend I did. Wouldn't you hate me for it?

GROUPER. How long would you be gone?

36

MYST. A month?

GROUPER. That wouldn't be so —

MYST. Two, maybe three.

GROUPER. That's the whole summer.

MYST. (*Lightly.*) We'd still have the winter, though, wouldn't we? That's the best time you said. Ghost Town.

GROUPER. Yeah. That's right.

MYST. You wouldn't love me by then, though, would you?

GROUPER. You know I would.

MYST. Really?

GROUPER. Yes.

MYST. (*Pause.*) I'm never going to forget you, Grouper.

GROUPER. You'll never be able to. I'll always be there.

MYST. (*About to say something, confide in him, but Myst pulls back and changes direction.*) What's the worst thing you ever did?

GROUPER. (*Taken aback.*) What?

MYST. The worst thing in your life.

GROUPER. Why?

MYST. Because I said so, that's why. Tell me something about you that really sucks.

GROUPER. Where should I start?

MYST. I'm serious.

GROUPER. You first. Give me inspiration.

MYST. I can't tell you the *worst* thing.

GROUPER. Why not?

MYST. I haven't done it yet. (*Smiles.*) Soon.

GROUPER. Great. Something to look forward to.

MYST. I can tell you a shitload of second worst things.

GROUPER. Okay. The atrocity hit parade.

MYST. Lemme see. Well, there was this one guy my mother lived with awhile, he owned a spa in New York. He was into all this kinky stuff, bondage and submission, and of course she'd tell me all about it, Snow the Leather Queen. She ate it up. Well, I was staying in the guest bedroom, right next to theirs, and I never could get any sleep. Every night it got worse and I had this cold that was driving me crazy and it was like living next to the Olympic Ring Team. And shit, my mother was in her thirties by then, *late* thirties —

GROUPER. Shit.

MYST. One time after I was up the whole night, I cornered this

37

clown in the hall. I told him I needed my sleep and gave him fifty bucks and told him to take my Mom to a motel. He thought I was kidding, being a smartass little kid. Just laughed at me. So I went into their bedroom and washed out his jar of vaseline, this big *vat* of it that was next to their bed, and filled it with my Vicks Vapo Rub.

GROUPER. I'm surprised that stopped her.

MYST. She was pretty worn out by then. She said I might have saved her life.

GROUPER. So that was a good deed. What about the bad things you did?

MYST. It's your turn.

GROUPER. Right.

MYST. The most despicable, ugly, self-hateable thing you've ever done.

GROUPER. You don't mean stuff I've been arrested for, then?

MYST. Not necessarily. Something *you* thought was bad.

GROUPER. I once had this jar of vapo-rub . . .

MYST. Funny.

GROUPER. (*Wanting to end the game.*) Come on, Myst. Cut it out —

MYST. All right. If you can't be honest with me.

GROUPER. I AM!

MYST. Well?

GROUPER. (*Pause.*) The worst thing I've ever done.

MYST. Right.

GROUPER. It's hard to narrow down.

MYST. I'll help. (*She smiles.*) What do you feel the most *guilty* over.

GROUPER. (*Pause.*) Seventh Grade. Larry Blume and his Superman suit.

MYST. Superman?

GROUPER. I hung around for awhile with this kid Larry Blume. He was the kind of kid who would read during lunch in the playground, you know? We only hung around together because nobody else would hang out with me. I'd either be getting into fights with them or their mothers told me I'd give them cooties or something. And nobody hung out with Blume because he was such a dork.

MYST. Fat?

GROUPER. Lousy in gym, too. He didn't stand a chance.

MYST. Go on.

GROUPER. I didn't realize this was an interrogation.

MYST. You got it.

GROUPER. Well. One day after school, Larry Blume tells me to come over to his house, he wants to show me something. This big secret, but I have to promise never to tell anybody.

MYST. You promised?

GROUPER. Of course I promised. I couldn't wait to see what he was so excited about. Blume was sweating heavy just talking about it. He made me wait in his bedroom, and he goes into the bathroom, and when he comes out Larry Blume is wearing this Superman suit, squinting like this . . . (*Demonstrates.*) 'cause he took his glasses off, and his belly's hanging over the Superman belt, but he's standing there with his hands on his hips, so happy with himself he can't stop grinning.

MYST. How old was he?

GROUPER. Twelve — thirteen.

MYST. Wow. Was he nuts?

GROUPER. Sure. HE was a friend of mine, wasn't he? I mean, nobody had even *read* a Superman comic book since second grade, and this chub ball's pretending to *be* him. He'd put on the outfit every day after school, lay on his bed and think about all the things he'd like to do to the kids who threw wet jawbreakers at him and called him Blume the Blimp and stuff. He said it would be our secret; we shook hands and the whole bit. He even asked me if I wanted to try on the suit.

MYST. Did you?

GROUPER. Are you warped? Anyhow, next day we're in the schoolyard at lunch, and somebody throws Blume's book over the fence. When he tried to get it, they got in this big circle, and kept pushing him back whenever he'd run for it. So he starts crying. Seventh Grade, and he's crying!

MYST. Yeah?

GROUPER. I just went crazy. I mean, if somebody busts your chops you either fight back or take it, but you don't cry — you don't let them know they're hurting you!

MYST. So?

GROUPER. So I shouted, "Fly and get it, Superman!" I screamed it, and Larry Blume looked over at me with this look

on his face, and the other kids, too, and somebody said "What?"
And they were all looking at me, sort of smiling, except Larry,
like "Us against Him, right?"

MYST. So you told them.

GROUPER. Yeah. Sure. (*Pause.*) Everybody laughed their
asses off and called Larry Super Blume and Clark Blimp and
that kind of stuff. (*Pause.*) Nice guy, right? Nice fucking guy.
And this was the only friend I had. (*Pause.*) You know what the
worst thing is? You wanted to know the worst thing, right,
Myst? I bet Blume could never put on that suit again.

MYST. Didn't he flip out? Jump out a window or something?

GROUPER. He wasn't that kind of kid.

MYST. What kind?

GROUPER. The jumping kind. He's probably graduating
from some prep school tonight, getting ready to major in law or
business and join the rifle club.

MYST. You're right, Grouper. That was pretty sleazy of you.

GROUPER. (*Getting angrier.*) Thank you. Thank you. You feel
bad enough about me now to be comfortable, Myst? Do you?
(*Walks away from her.*) Do we have any beer left?

MYST. One, I think.

GROUPER. It's mine. I'm taking it. (*Yells over cliff.*) I'M TAK-
ING THE LAST BEER! YOU KNOW ME, SELFISH, EVIL
AND THIRSTY! (*Drinks, pause. Turns to Myst.*) Why are you
so fucking quiet?

MYST. I'm not.

GROUPER. Good. 'Cause it's your turn. Let's go.

MYST. Forget it.

GROUPER. No way. Not after I scar somebody for life and
you save your Mother from being banged to death. Your turn.
You talk.

MYST. (*Trying to make light of it.*) Well. Once Mom got this
Americana attack and demanded I join Brownies. Threatened
to cut me out of the will. She wouldn't let me quit 'till I threw
half her record collection in the oven for a Brownie project and
made them into molded ashtrays. Hundreds of them, all around
the house.

GROUPER. (*Pause.*) That's cute. Very cute. Do you have any
stories *without* your mother?

MYST. (*Pause.*) Yeah. One time when I was just a little kid—

40

GROUPER. How old?

MYST. Nine—nine and a half, okay?

GROUPER. Okay.

MYST. I was staying at my aunt and uncle's house in Florida for the summer, and the big deal was that we were supposed to go to Disneyworld. I was all bent out of shape being there in the first place since my . . . since someone I won't mention didn't want me touring with her until I was older. Well, my cousin Jackie was eleven, and she was a real loser, but she had long blonde hair and she just got her first period, so my aunt and uncle were treating her like she found a cure for cancer. "My little girl's a woman now" and all that horse shit. I asked Jackie what this period stuff was, why she was a woman, and she said she was bleeding down there—bleeding from her "whatsee" as she so clinically described it. So I figured I could grow up fast and get out of Mousketeer land, and I got my uncle's razor that I saw my aunt use when she shaved her legs—another important ingredient to being a woman—I took the razor—

GROUPER. Don't Myst—(*Pause.*)

MYST. I bled real good. Mom came back from the tour and she was with me for almost two weeks. After that, we went to Disneyworld like crazy until Jackie was posing with Thumper and she said he felt her up. They said I almost died, but you know something, Grouper? (*Turns to him.*) It was wonderful. After I did it. The quiet. You're alone, but you're not lonely. Nothing to think about but watch your body try to breathe. You're awake but asleep at the same time. Awake inside but asleep outside, you know what I mean?

GROUPER. You were okay afterwards, though, weren't you?

MYST. You were just there, weren't you? No damaged goods, right? Best scissors and blue money could buy. Everything in working order. Everything. Working too well, maybe.

GROUPER. I thought these stories were supposed to be about what you did to somebody else.

MYST. Do you ever think of yourself that way? As somebody else? Somebody you can do anything to and nobody can stop you?

GROUPER. (*Pause.*) I'd stop you.

MYST. You would?

GROUPER. I swear.

41

MYST. Then I can count on you, right?

GROUPER. Right—

MYST. Just like Larry Blume did. Right, Group? Right, best friend?

GROUPER. (*Stunned.*) Why are you doing this?

MYST. Jesus, Grouper—stop fooling yourself. You'd dump on anybody to get what you want. The only things you care about are your little dreams—your stupid little fantasies that make you happy. Springsteen—Seaside—holding up in some fucking wasteland so nobody can get at you. You don't give a damn about anything else. (*She turns, walks away.*)

GROUPER. Myst, for Chrissake, will you get back here. I SAID GET BACK HERE!

MYST. (*Turns back to him.*) Fuck you! Who the hell are you to tell me anything?

GROUPER. Get a grip on yourself, will you?

MYST. Don't you dare say that to me, you asshole—

GROUPER. I'm not the one running around here throwing tantrums—you're being crazy!

MYST. You're a lot crazier than I am, Grouper, and you know it! You're fucking nuts!

GROUPER. I'm nuts? I'm not the one who bitches about her mom like a broken record and then can't wait to see her! You don't even like her!

MYST. So what? She likes me! That's more than you can say about your parents!

GROUPER. (*Grips his chest melodramatically.*) Zap! I'm heart-broken!

MYST. Screw you!

GROUPER. If your mom really loved you, don't you think she'd stop to see you more than once a year? Does she make only one tour in this area? Funny, all the times I've been in your room, the only times I've heard you talking to her is when *you* take three hours to track her down.

MYST. Why don't you jump, you piece of shit!

GROUPER. You first!

MYST. The only time I've ever seen your parents are in newspapers—

GROUPER. I don't *want* to see them—

42

MYST. —Newspapers on the wall of your room!

GROUPER. You know something? I think I'm all wrong about you.

MYST. You're all wrong, period. You couldn't love anybody! The only thing you could ever love is your retard brother because he's dumber than a stuffed animal!

GROUPER. You're a stupid, spoiled cunt—(*Grouper moves toward her; they edge around the car on opposite directions, moving the quickest when they near the edge.*)

MYST. And you're a lousy lay—

GROUPER. You're just a big hole, you know that? With every guy you meet pumping his shit into you. You're a garbage dump.

MYST. Oh yeah? Well a lot of people love to dump, and I loved all their garbage better than yours—

GROUPER. You're a whore—that's all you can ever be—a used up, cut up whore!

MYST. I loved Zeke, and Squirrel, and Flip and Jimmy Kay—

GROUPER. Shut up!

MYST. —And Jessie Dober, and Randy and Slingshot and Beanhead—

GROUPER. SHUT UP, I SAID—

MYST. AND MR. TRAVIS AND NICKY AND EVEN AMY TROY WAS BETTER THAN YOU, YOU FUCK-ING VIRGIN! (*Myst is shouting into Grouper's face. He leans back to hit her; both brace themselves. He veers from her to the hood of the car, slamming it over and over again.*) Don't Grouper. Don't. (*Hugs his back.*) Hit me instead. (*Grouper's stiff posture collapses. Pause. He pulls free of her.*)

GROUPER. (*Slowly.*) If we're going to the shore we have a five or six hour drive—

MYST. Grouper, we're not going to work out.

GROUPER. We will!

MYST. (*Pulls back from him.*) My stomach hurts. A lot. There's something wrong.

GROUPER. Sit down. Here. (*Sits her on hood.*)

MYST. O.K. I'm fine.

GROUPER. You want the rest of my beer?

MYST. (*Grimaces.*) God no.

GROUPER. Beer always makes my stomach feel better. Really.

43

It's better than Pepto Bismal. You don't throw up or anything. Just roll it around in your mouth 'till the cold is off, then let it slide down to your stomach. Try it—

MYST. (*She does.*) Thanks.

GROUPER. I love you.

MYST. Don't say that for awhile, all right?

GROUPER. That was our last fight.

MYST. Grouper; it wasn't our last and it wasn't even one of our best.

GROUPER. (*Ignoring her.*) I'm going to get gas. Then we're going to drive to Seaside. You can sleep in the back if you don't feel good—

MYST. I feel better. I feel fine. (*Jumps in back seat.*) How about one for the road?

GROUPER. Come on, Myst.

MYST. It would relax us!

GROUPER. I am relaxed! Why are you so nervous?

MYST. I'm not—

GROUPER. It's something!

MYST. (*Getting progressively more upset.*) This *is* sort of a big commitment, isn't it? Whether we get married or live together or even spend the summer together . . .

GROUPER. We're going to spend longer than that—

MYST. I've never made a commitment like this before to anybody. It's not that easy to do—

GROUPER. Myst, if the two of us can't commit to each other, who else could we ever commit to?

MYST. There are *so* many things that could go wrong!

GROUPER. (*Screams.*) I said you could fuck other guys, didn't I?

MYST. That's not it—

GROUPER. Your mom can visit anytime she wants—

MYST. I know that—

GROUPER. WHAT ELSE, THEN?

MYST. We could have a hard time finding a place to live—

GROUPER. We'll find a place. Worse comes to worse, we'll sleep on the beach—

MYST. (*Almost whiny.*) But that would be so—

GROUPER. WE'LL SLEEP IN THE CAR!

MYST. Maybe nobody will hire us. Singing or anything.

GROUPER. Somebody will. Besides, I have money, you have money — everybody we *know* has money.

MYST. You spend so much with all the shit you use —

GROUPER. TO PUT UP WITH YOU! (*Pause.*) We'll make it. And I could cut down —

MYST. I don't know if you'll be able to do that . . .

GROUPER. I swear, Myst. Trust me.

MYST. What if I get real out of control; who's going to keep an eye on me?

GROUPER. I will.

MYST. (*More and more upset.*) What if I'm sick?

GROUPER. I'll take you to a doctor.

MYST. What if I'm really sick? Are there good doctors there in wintertime?

GROUPER. I'LL TAKE YOU TO A HOSPITAL!

MYST. What if I'm pregnant? (*Pause.*) What if I was? What would you do about that? Get an abortion, right? Christ, abortions are no big deal. My mother has had more than I can count. I'm the only thing that squeezed by —

GROUPER. (*Quietly.*) Are you pregnant?

MYST. I said "What if" —

GROUPER. Myst —

MYST. I just wanted to see your reaction to it. I was making it up.

GROUPER. You're pregnant.

MYST. (*Pause.*) Yeah. (*She looks at him and becomes angry.*) I knew you'd react this way. Get all fucking hurt. I knew you'd make a big deal when it's no big thing. Shit. Sooner or later the odds get you, right? Your God of Math turns the numbers on you —

GROUPER. Who's the father?

MYST. Thanks a lot, Grouper. Count on you, right? Trust you, right? First thing you ask is who it was. YOUR feelings. You're some guy all right. Tell you what, you sit here in your car, and I'll go down to the station and have them send up gas and kleenex —

GROUPER. We can have the baby —

MYST. WE'RE not going to have anything! It's my baby! Fuck; I would have gone for a D & C this week except for graduation; there was so much to do with the packing and parties and everything. Even if I decided to have it I'd put it up for adoption; they're dying for white babies now, aren't they? They are. That's how we can make some quick bucks, right, Group? Sell it to the highest bidder: "How much for the grand kid of Snow Angeleeds."

GROUPER. If you keep the baby—

MYST. I'M NOT! (*Pause.*) Give me one good reason to keep it. Give me one good reason you'd want to see another baby in this world. What would you tell it, Grouper? What would you say is so wonderful about all this that it had to see? What's so wonderful about me . . . or you.

GROUPER. (*Pause.*) Then you'll get the abortion.

MYST. I KNOW I'LL GET IT. (*Pause.*) It's just going to be a little hard, you know . . . (*Begins to cry.*)

GROUPER. Myst—(*Reaches for her.*)

MYST. DON'T TOUCH ME! (*Long pause.*) You hate me, don't you?

GROUPER. No.

MYST. Hey; I'll get over it. You can get over anything, right?

GROUPER. I don't know.

MYST. I'm going to France with my mom, Group. It will be just for awhile.

GROUPER. (*Pause.*) Okay.

MYST. I'll be back. You let me know where you are, all right? I'll call you every day. Every day I can, anyhow. You go to Seaside, get a place, get a job, check out some of those bars, maybe—

GROUPER. Yeah. I could do that.

MYST. This is so fucking inconvenient, you know? I mean, what a pain in the ass way to ruin a graduation. When I told my mom—

GROUPER. She knows?

MYST. (*Pause.*) Yeah. She's in the middle of recording that record with Roger, but she came right out to the phone. She's wrapping it up next week, it's as soon as she could. She told me that a week or two wouldn't matter, though. She said to relax, it's no big deal.

GROUPER. She said that?

MYST. Shit, Grouper; she's right. Half the girls in our class have had abortions. I'm lucky it's only my first.

GROUPER. Myst. Let *me* help you. Let *me* do something for

you. If I'm no good to you, I'm no good to anybody.

MYST. You are helping me. You're helping by saying that.

GROUPER. That's not helping. That's just talking. (*Pause.*) I'm not enough, am I?

MYST. I don't know if anybody's enough for anybody, Grouper. Some people think they are, for awhile, but sooner or later they're on their own. Everybody's on their own.

GROUPER. I guess I was just being stupid.

MYST. No you weren't. You were just dreaming.

GROUPER. That's what I mean.

MYST. I love you, Grouper.

GROUPER. I love you too, Myst. (*Pause.*) That doesn't sound like anything at all. (*Sounds from below: the crackle of fireworks.*)

MYST. What's that?

GROUPER. A skyrocket, I think. Didn't Whorrie Laurie say she was going to have fireworks?

MYST. I think so. Hey; we have great seats for them, don't we? This is the first time I looked down on fireworks.

GROUPER. Climb up here. (*They get on hood of car.*)

MYST. I guess the party's almost over.

GROUPER. It's pretty late. (*Pause.*) Are you sorry you missed it?

MYST. Not at all. I had a wonderful night.

GROUPER. (*Pause.*) Myst; do you think that if we were in love for years and years that . . . things would change?

MYST. What do you mean?

GROUPER. Would I mean more to you? Would *anything* mean more?

MYST. I don't know. I mean, you look at people . . . I guess it depends on how stupid you get when you get older, whether things look better or not. I don't think things change. You can't stop shit from happening to you; you can't stop things hurting you.

GROUPER. Yes you can, Myst. You can. (*He stares at her; she meets his gaze, then looks away at the sound of another explosion.*)

MYST. (*Long pause.*) You can really see from here, can't you.

GROUPER. Yeah.

MYST. Are you okay?

GROUPER. Yeah. Just tired.

MYST. I guess we'd better call it a night.

GROUPER. We could never have a better night, do you think, Myst?

MYST. (*Meeting his stare.*) No. I don't think we ever could. (*They kiss.*) Happy graduation.

GROUPER. Happy graduation. (*He rises.*) Let's go. Give me your hand.

MYST. Can you see?

GROUPER. Yeah. Trust me.

MYST. Grouper, are you going to miss Seaside?

GROUPER. It could never be as good as I wanted it to be. How about France?

MYST. I've been there. No big deal.

GROUPER. No?

MYST. No. (*Myst puts up her hand; Grouper pulls her to his side.*) I love you Chauncey Morris.

GROUPER. I love you, Missy Angeleeds. (*Pause.*) On three. Ready?

MYST. Ready.

GROUPER. One—

MYST. Two—(*Clutching hands, they fly into the air. Blackout.*)

PROPERTY LIST

Parking barricade
Car
Joints
Pen & pencil set
Doll with hula skirt
Bottles of beer
Cassette tape
Colored underpants (2 pairs)
Watch

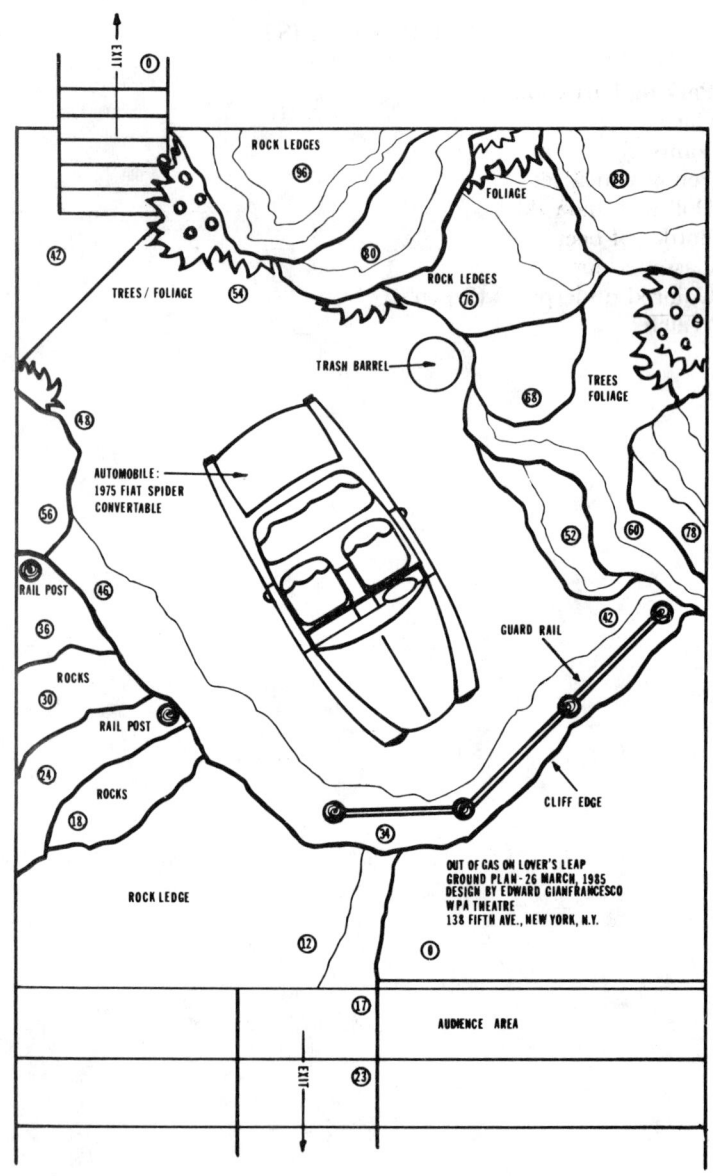

EXIT

ROCK LEDGES
96

58

FOLIAGE

42

80

TREES / FOLIAGE   54

ROCK LEDGES
76

TRASH BARREL

TREES
FOLIAGE

58

48

AUTOMOBILE:
1975 FIAT SPIDER
CONVERTABLE

56

52   60   78

RAIL POST   46

36

GUARD RAIL

42

ROCKS

30

RAIL POST

24

CLIFF EDGE

ROCKS

18

34

OUT OF GAS ON LOVER'S LEAP
GROUND PLAN - 26 MARCH, 1985
DESIGN BY EDWARD GIANFRANCESCO
WPA THEATRE
138 FIFTH AVE., NEW YORK, N.Y.

ROCK LEDGE

12

0

17   AUDIENCE AREA

EXIT   23

50

At The End of Every Tunnel

music Lucy Simon
lyric Mark St. Germain

© Calougie Music, Ascap
1985

NEW PLAYS

★ **SHEL'S SHORTS by Shel Silverstein.** Lauded poet, songwriter and author of children's books, the incomparable Shel Silverstein's short plays are deeply infused with the same wicked sense of humor that made him famous. "...[a] childlike honesty and twisted sense of humor." *—Boston Herald.* "...terse dialogue and an absurdity laced with a tang of dread give [*Shel's Shorts*] more than a trace of Samuel Beckett's comic existentialism." *—Boston Phoenix.* [flexible casting] ISBN: 0-8222-1897-6

★ **AN ADULT EVENING OF SHEL SILVERSTEIN by Shel Silverstein.** Welcome to the darkly comic world of Shel Silverstein, a world where nothing is as it seems and where the most innocent conversation can turn menacing in an instant. These ten imaginative plays vary widely in content, but the style is unmistakable. "...[*An Adult Evening*] shows off Silverstein's virtuosic gift for wordplay...[and] sends the audience out...with a clear appreciation of human nature as perverse and laughable." *—NY Times.* [flexible casting] ISBN: 0-8222-1873-9

★ **WHERE'S MY MONEY? by John Patrick Shanley.** A caustic and sardonic vivisection of the institution of marriage, laced with the author's inimitable razor-sharp wit. "...Shanley's gift for acid-laced one-liners and emotionally tumescent exchanges is certainly potent..." *—Variety.* "...lively, smart, occasionally scary and rich in reverse wisdom." *—NY Times.* [3M, 3W] ISBN: 0-8222-1865-8

★ **A FEW STOUT INDIVIDUALS by John Guare.** A wonderfully screwy comedy-drama that figures Ulysses S. Grant in the throes of writing his memoirs, surrounded by a cast of fantastical characters, including the Emperor and Empress of Japan, the opera star Adelina Patti and Mark Twain. "Guare's smarts, passion and creativity skyrocket to awesome heights..." *—Star Ledger.* "...precisely the kind of good new play that you might call an everyday miracle...every minute of it is fresh and newly alive..." *—Village Voice.* [10M, 3W] ISBN: 0-8222-1907-7

★ **BREATH, BOOM by Kia Corthron.** A look at fourteen years in the life of Prix, a Bronx native, from her ruthless girl-gang leadership at sixteen through her coming to maturity at thirty. "...vivid world, believable and eye-opening, a place worthy of a dramatic visit, where no one would want to live but many have to." *—NY Times.* "...rich with humor, terse vernacular strength and gritty detail..." *—Variety.* [1M, 9W] ISBN: 0-8222-1849-6

★ **THE LATE HENRY MOSS by Sam Shepard.** Two antagonistic brothers, Ray and Earl, are brought together after their father, Henry Moss, is found dead in his seedy New Mexico home in this classic Shepard tale. "...His singular gift has been for building mysteries out of the ordinary ingredients of American family life..." *—NY Times.* "...rich moments ...Shepard finds gold." *—LA Times.* [7M, 1W] ISBN: 0-8222-1858-5

★ **THE CARPETBAGGER'S CHILDREN by Horton Foote.** One family's history spanning from the Civil War to WWII is recounted by three sisters in evocative, intertwining monologues. "...bittersweet music—[a] rhapsody of ambivalence...in its modest, garrulous way...theatrically daring." *—The New Yorker.* [3W] ISBN: 0-8222-1843-7

★ **THE NINA VARIATIONS by Steven Dietz.** In this funny, fierce and heartbreaking homage to *The Seagull,* Dietz puts Chekhov's star-crossed lovers in a room and doesn't let them out. "A perfect little jewel of a play..." *—Shepherdstown Chronicle.* "...a delightful revelation of a writer at play; and also an odd, haunting, moving theater piece of lingering beauty." *—Eastside Journal (Seattle).* [1M, 1W (flexible casting)] ISBN: 0-8222-1891-7

DRAMATISTS PLAY SERVICE, INC.
440 Park Avenue South, New York, NY 10016 212-683-8960 Fax 212-213-1539
postmaster@dramatists.com www.dramatists.com